Wonders *of the* Horus Temple

Wonders *of the* Horus Temple

The Sound and Light of Edfu

Introduced by
Zahi Hawass

Photographs by
Sherif Sonbol

Misr Company for Sound, Light, & Cinema—Cairo
Distributed by the American University in Cairo Press

Page 2: The first hypostyle hall

Page 4: Statue of Horus at the pylon entrance to the Temple of Horus

Dar el Kutub No. 14082/10
ISBN 978 977 638 900 7

Dar el Kutub Cataloging-in-Publication Data

Hawass, Zahi
        Wonders of the Horus Temple: The Sound and Light of Edfu/ Introduced by Zahi Hawass.
    First Edition.—Cairo: The American University in Cairo Press, 2010

        96p.   cm.
        ISBN 978 977 638 900 7
        1. Theater—sound effects   2. Pyramids—Egypt
        I. Hawass, Zahi, 1947 (intro)
        792-024

1 2 3 4 5 6 7 8   14 13 12 11 10

Distributed by the American University of Cairo Press
113 Sharia Kasr el Aini, Cairo, Egypt
420 Fifth Avenue, New York, NY 10018
www.aucpress.com

Designed by Adam el Sehemy
Printed in Egypt

Contents

Preface

A new pearl has joined our necklace of sound and light projects, deployed at a number of Egyptian monuments and antiquity areas: the Sound and Light Show at the Temple of Horus at Edfu.

Given the historical and antique importance of the temple of Edfu, its integrated and magnificent architecture, and the high demand from visitors by land and Nile cruise on their way to Luxor and Aswan, the idea of establishing a sound and light show project at this great temple was appealing. Edfu is located halfway between Luxor and Aswan, and most boats harbor at Edfu to avoid sailing at night and to visit the temple.

Both mythical and historical characters, such as the god Horus, the goddess Hathor, the priest, the archaeologist in charge of the temple, and the king, participate in presenting the show. The show tells the story of the life of Horus and his mother Isis, and their war and triumph over the god of evil, Set. It also tells of the romance of Horus and Hathor, their annual cruise in the Nile, and the annual celebration of the victory of Horus.

The show consists of three phases. The first starts at the pharaonic hill site, at the pharaonic exhibition, after the audience enters the temple from

1

the rear at the northern pylon. Here, the audience sees a view of the temple followed by the story of its building and its history.

Then, the audience walks through the corridors and passageways of the temple into the open court, to watch the second phase of the show, characterized by music and lights. They continue walking until they reach the columns with the botanical capitals on three sides of the temple, where they stand to follow the show. In the back of the temple, the audience can see other architectural aspects of the temple, like the courtyard, the hypostyle hall established on twelve columns, with two granite statues of the god Horus in the shape of a falcon, another hall with twelve columns, and two rooms on opposite sides—one used as a library and the second for preserving religious ritual tools and vessels. The visitors then go into two lobbies, the first called the sacrifice hall and the other the resting place of the god. Then they enter the holy of holies, where there is a granite naos, dedicated to the god Horus, with the sacred bark in front of it. The holy of holies is surrounded by twelve rooms, their walls engraved with religious images and inscriptions. The roof has gargoyles in the form of lions.

During this phase, the audience learns about the priests' daily rituals: the commoners were banned from entering this area.

Finally, the audience leaves through the open court in the direction of main building for the third and last phase of the show where they watch the story of the temple, the rituals, and the gods on huge images covering the right and left surfaces of the pylon.

A large amount of technical equipment is used to amaze the audience and at the same time maintain the environment and integrity of the archaeological site. The most important pieces of equipment are four high-definition video projectors, three movable overhead projectors, used for the first time in sound and light shows to give a special dazzling effect, 258 LED lighting units, and forty sound speakers.

Eng. Essam Abdel Hadi
Chairman and Managing Director
Misr Company for Sound, Light, and Cinema

Acknowledgments

Main Contractor and Technical Installations
Horizon for Trading and Contracting
Wael Gouda, project manager

Artistic Directors, Visuals, Lighting
Casa Magica
Friedrich Förster and Sabine Weissinger

Creative Crew
Siegfried Bühr and Oliver Moumouris, dramatic structure, script
Stephan Böhme de Marco, composition and music/sound production
Bernhard Höfert, lighting design

Scientific Consultant
Prof. Dieter Kurth

Executive Engineers
Fawzi Ahmad Abd al-Hamid
Muhammad Raafat Abdalla Shaeer
Khaled Mousa
Inji Ibrahim

Technical Team
Ibrahim Badri
Ayman Abu al-Magd

Cairo Opera House Team
Muhammad Hamdi, head of the Technical Musical Committee

Horus and the
Temple of Edfu

Zahi Hawass

I n 1969, when I was a young man working as an inspector of antiquities at Tuna al-Gebel, I was sent to work at the site of Edfu for three
months. I did not know anyone at Edfu, so most of my time was spent
inspecting the archaeological sites around it. One of the most important
sites in this area is Nekhen, which the Greeks called Hierakonpolis, and
which is known today as Kom al-Ahmar. It was one of the most important
religious sites of the Predynastic era, and its patron deity was Horus. The
temple of Edfu, some sixteen kilometers south of Hierakonpolis, was also
significant in ancient Egypt, and was another site of worship for Horus.
While I was working there, I used to visit the temple at sunrise and sunset.
I would go to the top of the temple and sit in this beautiful place and watch
the sky and think.

There were three issues about the site of Edfu that troubled me at the
time. The first was that visitors entered the temple from the back and not
through the main entrance, as in pharaonic times. The second was that the
people who sold souvenirs displayed their wares in an unorganized way on
the street, and also the cafeteria on site did not suit the temple area at all.
The third issue was that most of the cruise boats arrived in Edfu at night,

meaning that travelers would visit the temple at night, before or after dinner, or at sunrise. I decided that this location needed a Sound and Light project, because it could be an enjoyable event for all visitors to the town of Edfu.

When I became secretary general of the Supreme Council of Antiquities, one of my goals was to save this beautiful temple. We began to implement a site-management program, and for three years I visited the temple at least once a month in order to review the progress myself. We changed the way people enter the temple: they now enter through the main entrance that was used in the time of the pharaohs. In the area in front of the temple we built shops and rented them to the people who sell souvenirs and closed off the unsightly area at the back of the temple. And we built a road west of the temple and a parking lot outside it to facilitate visits to the temple.

We also created a beautiful open-air museum garden on the west side of the temple, where visitors can sit and observe the beauty of the most complete and well-preserved temple in Egypt. Also, for the first time the site is

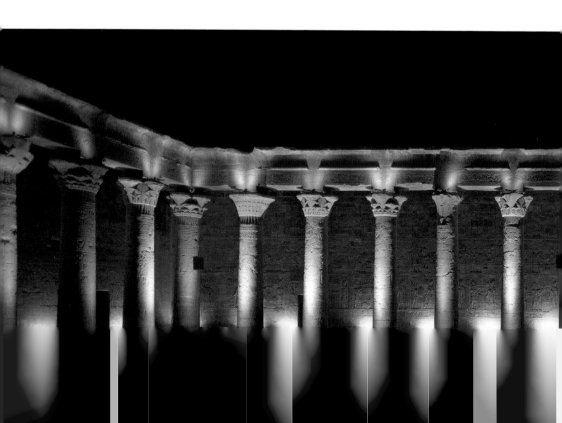

equipped with excellent visitor facilities, including cafeterias, shops, and clean restrooms. The most important part is the visitor center, which features a film about the temple and the site of Edfu, produced by the National Geographic Society and narrated by my great friend, the famous Egyptian actor, Omar Sharif.

I am happy that the Sound and Light Show now takes place inside the temple and with new technology. When I wrote the script for the show I imagined how, with modern technology, we would be able to see Hathor, the ancient Egyptian goddess of love and beauty, as she left her temple in Dendera and traveled south to visit her husband Horus in Edfu.

The temple's open court was used for many festivals throughout the year, and also served as a place for delegates from foreign countries to meet. This court was the place of ritual meeting for Horus of Edfu and his wife, Hathor of Dendera. This is reflected in the scenes carved into the court's walls of "The Feast of the Beautiful Meeting" and also the "court of

offerings." The first hypostyle hall contains twelve large columns, as well as scenes of the temple's foundation and construction. The most important of these scenes shows the king leaving his palace with the goddess of writing, Seshat, in order to lay out the foundations for the temple. This hall would also have contained the temple's archives. Other rooms include the "Nile room," which contained the ritual water for purification, and the "laboratory room," where oils and incense were prepared to anoint the bodies of the gods. The most important, and secret, room in the temple was the sanctuary, *set weret* or the 'great throne.' Only the king or the high priest could enter this sanctuary where the god Horus resided.

The temple of Edfu may be best known for its depictions of numerous feasts and festivals, such as the New Year's Festival, the Feast of the Beautiful Meeting, and the Festival of Victory. This celebration commemorated Horus's victory over his nemesis, Seth. In addition to scenes of this festival, the temple of Edfu also has the most complete depiction of the battles between Horus and Seth, including vignettes of Horus smiting Seth, who appears in the form of a hippopotamus.

I recommend that everyone visit this temple when they travel to Egypt. I believe that when people come to Edfu they will experience the magic of the site.

History of the Site

Early evidence of occupation at Edfu dates from the Old Kingdom necropolis located between the Ptolemaic temple and the Muslim cemetery. This cemetery contains many mastabas in the southwest area, near the temple, one of which belonged to Isi, who was the mayor of the area at the beginning of the Sixth Dynasty. In the Middle Kingdom, Isi was worshiped as a living god. This area was the location of tomb stelae dating from the Sixth Dynasty to the Thirteenth Dynasty. Before the beginning of the New Kingdom, the cemeteries were moved to another site called Hagar Edfu, which is located four kilometers west of the temple, and in the Late Period to Nag al-Hissaya about twelve kilometers to the south. The remains of the ancient city are about 150 meters west of the temple.

For most of its history, Edfu was the capital of the second nome, or district of Upper Egypt and was known in Ptolemaic times as Apollinopolis Magna, 'the great city of Apollo,' not to be confused with Apollinopolis Parva, 'the small town of Apollo,' located at modern-day Qus. The ancient religious name of Edfu was Behdet, because the local god was Hor-Behdety, who was worshiped there along with the god Horus in his form as a solar god. The Greeks connected Horus with their god Apollo. In Coptic, the area was called Atbu or Atfu, from which the modern name, Edfu, derives. The Temple of Edfu played an important role in the religious life of the ancient Egyptians, and was also a center for science and knowledge.

After the decline of the ancient Egyptian religion in the fourth century AD, the temple began to be visited again at the end of the sixteenth century by European travelers. Richard Lepsius, the great German archaeologist, discovered a text in the middle of the nineteenth century called the temple documents, recorded on the limestone wall of the temple. Lepsius copied the text and Auguste Mariette began to clear the temple of sand in 1860. The first scientific publication was begun by Maxence de Rochemonteix in 1876, and the most complete records were made by Emile Chassinat, published in fourteen parts between 1897 and 1934. Recently, more accurate publications by Sylvie Cauville and Dieter Kurth have become increasingly important.

The Supreme Council of Antiquities also carried out excavations on the west side of the temple, which was made rather difficult because more of the site was buried under modern houses. The archaeological site includes: the temple of Horus, the necropolis of al-Aasaia located four kilometers southwest of Edfu with rock-cut tombs dating to the Late Period, the Ptolemaic tombs, and the village of Hush, which includes a group of quarries dated to the pharaonic and Greek periods.

The Temple of Horus

The temple of Horus, located about one hundred kilometers south of Luxor, on the west bank of the Nile, is the most important site one can visit in the city of Edfu. It is the best preserved temple from ancient Egypt, largely because it was buried by sand in antiquity and remained mostly covered until 1860, when Auguste Mariette began to clear the sand away.

Stages of Construction of the Temple

It is clear that this temple was small in the pharaonic period and then expanded greatly during the Ptolemaic period. Texts on the walls of the temple of Edfu record that the current building was started in the reign of Ptolemy III in the third month of the summer season of 237 BC and was constructed over a period of 180 years. The temple was finally finished in 57 BC, during the reign of Ptolemy XII, the father of Cleopatra VII, and it remained in use until the Roman period. The high priest responsible for the inscriptions and the design left a text in the year 100 BC written on the outer façade of the outer temple wall. The text covers a three-hundred-square-meter space on the wall and explains the construction of the temple in detail. The priest who wrote it described the temple as the most beautiful temple ever built. He recorded the names of the temple and the names of the kings who participated in the construction.

The construction and inscription ended in the twenty-fifth year of the reign of Ptolemy XII, on 5 December 57 BC. The whole length of the temple is 137 meters. Additions were made to the temple during the Roman period in two locations, one north of the door that leads to the *mammisi* and the second on the south side of the western tower of the pylon. The pylon bore the traditional scenes of the king smiting his enemies, which was part of the political program that assured his divinity, by carrying out his duty to protect Egypt from its enemies.

The God Horus-Behdety

The main god of the temple was a version of Horus named after the city: Horus of Behdet. Horus is one of the best-known gods of the ancient Egyptian pantheon and was the first public god of the state after the unification of Egypt. He was a sky deity, with his left eye representing the moon and his right eye the sun. Horus is the Latin version of the word *Hr*, which means face, and indeed Horus took many faces, most commonly appearing as a hawk or a human with the head of a hawk. In the Greco-Roman period, Horus the Child came to be called Harpocrates. The main centers of worship of Horus were at Hierakonpolis, Dendera, Edfu, and Kom Ombo.

The Temple Plan

Edfu is the largest temple in Egypt after Karnak; it is 137 meters long, thirty-six meters wide, and it covers an area of seven thousand square meters. The temple complex includes a sacred lake, a place for the slaughter of animals for offerings and the feast, a sacred area for the raising of the sacred hawks, and houses for the priests. The main entrance of Edfu temple is located on a north-south axis and the entire site is surrounded by an enclosure wall.

The temple proper is fronted with the two towers of the pylon that reach about thirty-six meters in height and sixty-four meters in width. The pylon had niches for the flags of the gods to be flown from flagpoles. After the pylon is the gate of the large temple, which had a door made of cedar wood, covered with gold and bronze decoration and topped with a sun disk. In front of the temple entrance are two colossal granite hawk statues, which symbolize the god Horus wearing the double crown of Upper and Lower Egypt.

The most important scene on the front of the pylon is a scene of Ptolemy XII smiting his enemies in the presence of Horus, Lord of Edfu, and Hathor, Lady of Dendera. Above this scene on the two pylon towers is a scene of the king giving offerings to a number of gods in two rows. The back of the pylon contains scenes of the rituals of the temple construction. Here we see the king outside the palace, wearing the white crown of Upper Egypt; in front of him are a priest burning incense and four gods: this scene depicts the purification of the king by Thoth, Horus, Nekhbet, and Wadjet. Also shown is the coronation of the king with the crowns of Upper and Lower Egypt while Horus holds the royal scepter in the presence of Atum, Seshat, and Maat, and the king stands in front of Horus and Hathor. Below are scenes of the Nile festival, when Hathor comes from Dendera to meet her husband, Horus.

The pylon gate opens onto a large peristyle court with thirty-two pillars that have capitals in the form of lotus flowers and papyrus plants. The peristyle court was used for feasts and festivals. One of the names of this court is "the place of meeting," and another is "the court of offering." There are scenes of the king giving offerings to the gods. On the right side he is shown wearing the white crown of Upper Egypt and on the left he wears the red crown of Lower Egypt.

On the wall behind the rows of pillars are a number of scenes of the king performing religious rituals and an offering inscription of a king whose name is not known. This pillared hall leads to two doors on the eastern wall and two doors on the western wall. The most important space was the area in the southeast corner that was used by Hathor during the festival of the sacred marriage when she ritually traveled from Dendera to Edfu.

The first, or outer, hypostyle hall is called the Hall of the Great Rulers. It is the highest and widest point of the temple, and contains twelve pillars. On the façade of the hall we see the king in front of Horus in the festival when the stone foundation of the temple was laid. Its walls are decorated with scenes of the temple foundation ceremony and other traditional scenes. The most important scene shows the king leaving his palace with the goddess Seshat, the goddess of writing, as she prepares the land for the construction of the temple. Here she performs several rituals, including purifying the land for the temple, raising the first piece of stone, censing the temple, and consecrating the site as a gift to Horus. Another scene depicts the king using an adze to work the land and also making a mud brick and placing it in the foundation deposit; the scene ends with the king giving offerings to Horus. Other scenes show the king performing rituals as high priest in the festival of Horus and Hathor. The first hypostyle court contained the temple library. Conveniently, there is a record of all the volumes kept in the library because their titles were inscribed on the temple walls. This hall also contains the entrance to the robing room, which is similar to the one found at the temple of Hathor at Dendera.

The first hypostyle hall is followed by the second hypostyle hall, which also has twelve pillars, but is narrower than the first hall. Leading off of the second hypostyle hall are entrances to the Nile room, which held a reservoir of pure water for purification, and the laboratory room, where recipes for oils and ointments that were used on the statue of the god, Amun, are inscribed on the walls. According to ancient records, it was a secret place that "no one sees and no one hears"; it was meant to contain secret knowledge that was only accessible by the lector priests. The treasure room, also accessible from the second hypostyle hall, was used for the storage of gold, silver, and precious stones. The scenes here are similar to those found in the first hypostyle hall, but the king in the inscriptions is Ptolemy IV instead of Ptolemy III. Scenes in this hypostyle hall also depict the sacred feast.

After the second hypostyle hall is the Hall of Offering built by Ptolemy IV for various gods, as well as his parents, Ptolemy III and Berenike II. On the eastern and western sides of this hall are staircases which lead up to the roof of the temple. Scenes on the stairways depict different gods climbing the stairs. There is also a scene of Cleopatra II holding a sistrum, and Ptolemy II and Ptolemy IV burning incense in the presence of the Edfu triad, while before them stand the gods Ihy, Khonsu, Isis, and others.

The Hall of Offering opens onto the main sanctuary, the holy of holies, which is surrounded by ten smaller chapels dedicated to various deities, including Osiris, Ra, Hathor, and Khonsu. On the western side, one chapel is dedicated to the god of fertility, Min, while on the eastern side of the sanctuary another chapel is dedicated to Nut, the goddess of the sky, who is depicted on the ceiling with her body stretched above a number of boats, one holding the sun god.

The sanctuary was known as *set weret*, which means 'the great throne,' and was only entered by the king or the high priest. Inside this sanctuary was located the sacred bark of the god and a naos, or shrine, for a golden statue of the god. The holy of holies, the most sacred space in the temple, has scenes of the sacred boat of Horus, and shown in front of the naos is the king in three different poses and a scene of the sacred boat of Hathor.

The holy of holies faces south, and was surrounded by an ambulatory passageway and smaller chapels on the west, east, and north sides, which is typical of ancient Egyptian temples from the pharaonic period. Edfu also has a wall surrounding the central structure, creating another passageway outside the temple. The interior façade of this wall contains the scenes of the battle of Horus and Seth. On the eastern and western sides, there are scenes of Horus slaughtering the enemies of Ra, represented as crocodiles and hippopotami. On the western and northern sides are scenes of a sledge that holds the boat of Horus with the king inside, slaying a hippo with an arrow. To the south of this scene is a sailboat with Isis kneeling on the front, holding the hippo with a rope while Horus stands at the back shooting his arrow into the neck of the animal. At that point, the passage narrows, and there is an interesting scene of three people, the first killing a hippo with a knife, the second labeled as Imhotep, reading a papyrus scroll, and the third holding a goose for sacrifice. There are also scenes of Horus Sematawy, the son of Edfu, holding a finger to his mouth.

The Mammisi

The *mammisi* was a Greco-Roman addition to ancient Egyptian temples, a development of the concept from the pharaonic period, when a specific room was set aside for the festival of the god of the temple. An example is from Deir al-Bahari, where the divine birth of Hatshepsut is depicted. The *mammisi* at Edfu is located just south of the temple entrance, and was begun by Ptolemy VIII and Ptolemy IX. It is a rectangular structure consisting of a room decorated with scenes of the sacred birth, including a scene of the god being nursed by Hathor. It is dedicated to Horus, Hathor, and their son Ipi/Harsomptus.

The Festivals of the Temple

Inscriptions throughout the temple depict the important feasts and festivals celebrated at Edfu, including the New Year's Festival, the Behdet feast that celebrated the day Hathor traveled from Dendera to Edfu to visit Horus, and the feast of the Crowning of the Hawk. The most important festival depiction portrays the legend of Horus and Seth, and Horus's victory festival, which was acted out as a play near the sacred lake.

The Festival of the New Year was celebrated at the time when the flood-waters began to rise, marking the renewal of life and the fertility of the land. The Festival of the Crowning of the Sacred Hawk was celebrated on the fifth day of the first month of winter.

The Festival of Victory, which was celebrated beginning on the twenty-first day of the second month of winter, commemorated the victory of Horus over Seth. As part of the festivities, the local people would re-enact the battle in a play. The play included the important scenes from the mythological battle, in order to ritually ensure the continued victory of Horus over Seth.

The last festival celebrated the sacred marriage of Horus and Hathor. It was first celebrated during the reign of Thutmose III and continued into the Greco-Roman period. The thirteenth-day festival marked the journey of Hathor from Dendera to Edfu in order to consecrate their marriage. This festival usually coincided with celebrations of the harvest, because of its symbolic connections to fertility.

The great pylon of the Temple of Horus

The peristyle court

Above: Horus on the pylon façade

Right: Horus in front of the first hypostyle hall

Below: The sacred boats of Horus and Hathor

Left: Hathor and Horus

Above: Detail of the hieroglyphs

The king accompanies
Hathor's sacred boat

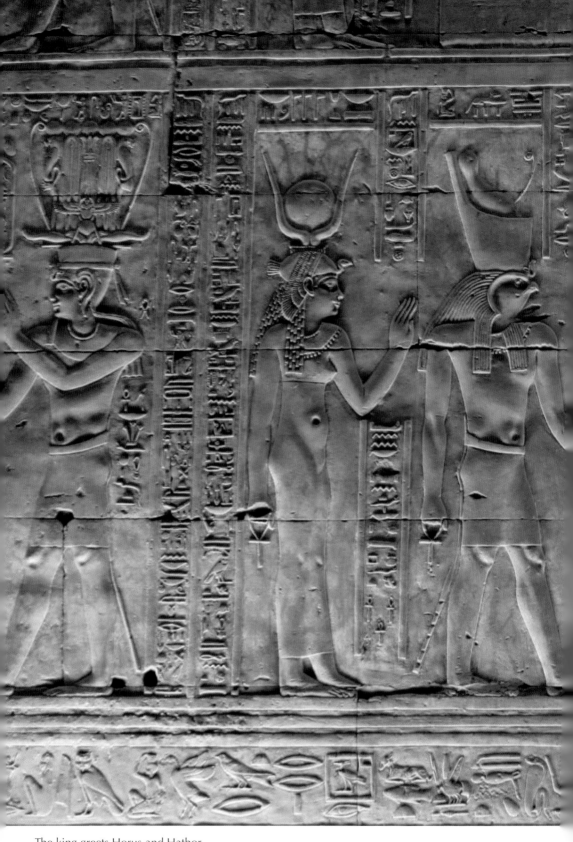

The king greets Horus and Hathor

The temple of Horus at Edfu

Hathor and Horus receive
offerings from the king

Above: The king makes an offering to Horus

Above and below: Hieroglyphs on the walls of the temple

The sanctuary, or
holy of holies

Following pages: The mammisi

The corridor around the sanctuary

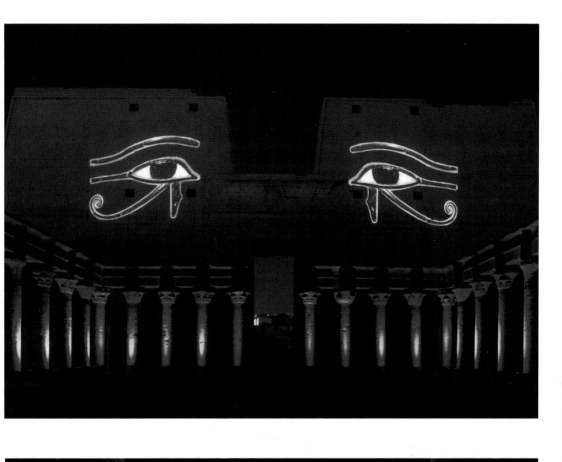

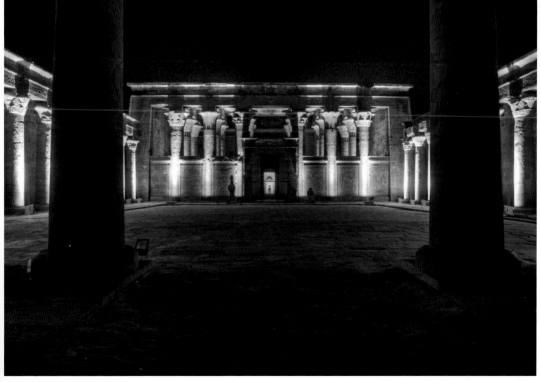

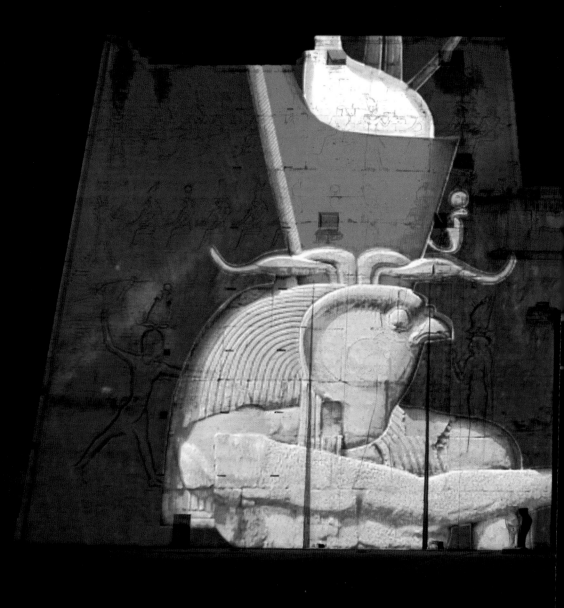

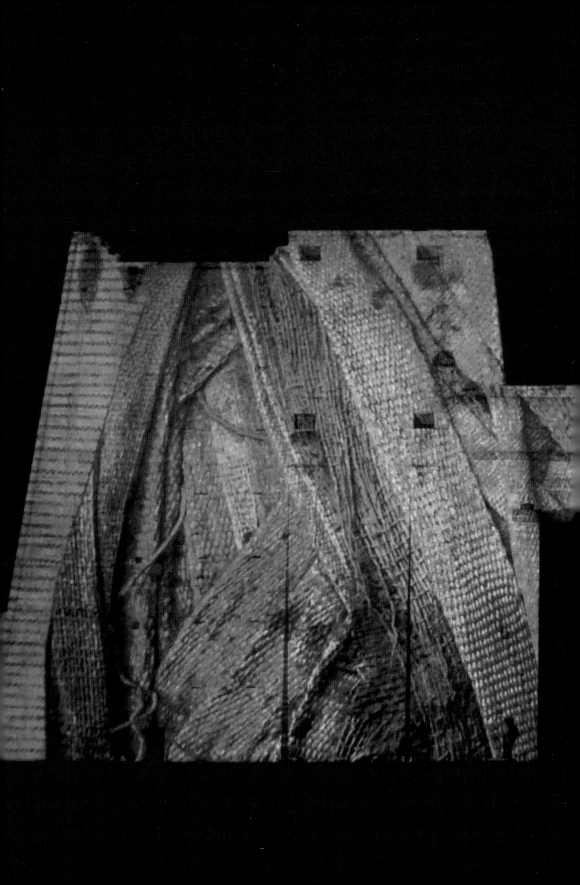

Sound and Light at the
Horus Temple in Edfu

SALUTATION AND INVOCATION
Temple guide
Welcome, journeyers, here in this perfect place which lies before you like the sleeping body of a god—grandly bearing witness to the time which these walls have outlasted.

This temple likens a book. If you know how to read its scripture, its images, it will open up like a gate to the past, a gate to the day, night, and rebirth of all that is alive.

Priest
May Horus live, with godly body, the perfect youngling, Favored-by-All, whom his mother Isis brought to splendor on the throne of his father Osiris.

Long live the King of Upper and Lower Egypt, loved by Horus-Behdety, the Great God and Lord of Heaven in Edfu.

This perfect place is his horizon on earth, the house in which his majesty appears, in which he awakens in the morning and reposes in the evening.

The place in which his body has been nourished from the very beginning, the grave of the One-with-Dappled-Plumage, the Grand Site of the greatest of the gods.

Expert

The temple—it is an edifice built by humans and a godly dwelling alike—that of Horus, the falcon-like god.

Here he lives among human beings, Horus-Behdety, the source and shelter of all that is alive. He assures a pleasant life, he loves justice, order, truth. He revels in the good measure of all things, in Maat!

In the House of the Large Winged Disc of Edfu there is also room for all the other gods. But here, Horus is the grandest among them; he is the Lord of House.

HISTORY
Commentator A

Three-hundred and thirty-two before the common era.

Commentator B

Alexander the Great takes over Egypt from the Persian rule.

A new age is ushered in: Hellenism.

The new capital, Alexandria, is founded.

Alexander is convinced of his godly origin: he ascends the pharaoh's throne.

Commentator A

Three-hundred and twenty-three before the common era.

Commentator B

Alexander the Great is dead.

The Macedonian empire collapses and the Greek governor Ptolemy becomes the first new ruler of Egypt. The age of the Ptolemaic Dynasty begins.

The Egyptian empire experiences its last Golden Age, reaches its largest territorial expansion.

Commentator A

Two-hundred and thirty-seven before the common era.

Commentator B

Ptolemy the Third is the ruler who founds the new Horus Temple in Edfu, the most magnificent religious edifice of Ptolemaic Egypt perfectly built in the ancient Egyptian style.

Commentator A

Fifty-seven before the common era, after a construction period of 180 years, the temple in Edfu is finally completed.

THE BUILDING INSCRIPTION
Temple guide

. . . and here on the enclosure wall, the temple's own building history is written onto its skin . . .

Priest

These are the superb monuments which His Majesty and his father created.

Their names were engraved with ore to lend them permanence so future generations can pay tribute to their perfection.

Oh, you kings of Upper and Lower Egypt! May your images be indestructible on earth and your heirs be secure on your throne!

Expert

The entire temple was fashioned in the most beautiful way, with engraved inscriptions, the walls embellished with gold, and colors laid on.

The decoration as a whole was executed in accordance with the scriptures. The papyrus rolls lie in the library and each ritual takes place as prescribed.

INVITATION TO ENTER THE TEMPLE
Temple guide

Horus beheld his temple, opened his mouth, and spoke to the gods of his following.

Horus

Let us enter so that we take possession of the Nome-of-the-Gods which our hearts long for; for this is the sublime place where we want to take up residence, our place to dwell on earth.

Expert

In ancient times only the king and the priests were permitted to enter the interior of the temple.

Temple guide

But today, you are granted this opportunity as well!

Come! Enter the place where the heart of the falcon beats.

The Rituals in the Temple
MYTH OF CREATION
Horus

I have opened your heart.

You have come so that your heart be placed in the right spot.

You should breathe in life through the one who was envisioned between the primeval ocean and heaven among the first reeds.

THE MORNING RITUAL
Alternating priests

I have ascended the steps, I have approached the boat with the name Bearer-of-Beauty so as to see the god in his barge with my hands clean, my feet flawless, and my whole body consecrated.

I have pulled the cord away to approach the shrine. I open the wing of the door at the Horizon-of-Re so as to banish the darkness from the sun disc which is inside.

I have undone the seal so as to hold high the Living Eye for his lord. I am Thoth, who brings the Brilliant Eye to his lord and makes Horus satisfied.

You radiate on earth just like you appear in the sky, and your radiant light besprinkles the entire world. The gods revive and praise your beauty!

I have beheld the god, the Powerful One is beholding me. The god rejoices at the sight of me as soon as I behold the statue of the godly winged scarab, the sublime figure of the Falcon-of-Gold.

THE MORNING HYMN
Voices alternating and together

Awake peacefully, may you awake well and in peace. Awake, Horus-Behdety, with life.

May both your Living Eyes, sun and moon, awake in peace, send out fire and banish the dark.

May your eyebrows, which make your face cheerful and know no anger, awake in peace.

May your nose, the nest of the air with which you breathe, awake in peace.

May your lips, the two-door leaves of heaven which you open so that the land lives, awake in peace.

May your tongue, which speaks life time and again, which speaks fair judgments, awake in peace.

May both your wings of Behdety, with which you fly above the sky-goddess Nut, awake in peace.

May your body awake in peace with all that is in it, that is the sky studded with its stars!

DAILY LIFE OF THE TEMPLE
Expert
The priests have paid homage to the god and honored him, thereupon they offered him food and drink.

After the god is invigorated, the priests and the rest of the temple personnel consume the offerings in an adjoining room of the temple.

After the morning repast it is time for the toilet, the statue is washed and anointed, dressed splendidly, coiffured and decorated with jewels.

But life around the temple has begun much earlier. Even before dawn there was work to do: bread was baked, animals butchered, the offering of food for the god prepared.

The entire premises of the temple were a lively enterprise with substantial property, agriculture, workshops, laboratories, and offices. Thus the august priests, the highest of whom was the king himself, were not the only ones belonging to the temple but also farmers, craftsmen, scribes, medical men, and clerks. The temple dictated the rhythm of life in Edfu from morning until evening.

As soon as the sun sets, Horus-Behdety is prepared for the night.

The Evening Ritual
THE SAFEGUARD OF THE NIGHT
Priest

I have come to you, Great Falcon, as Re is now descending in the west and I am equipped with everything needed to protect your house, your bed chamber, and your residence.

I ignite the torches and surround your house with the magnificent tutelary goddesses of Re and Osiris.

I decorate your forehead with a band of king's linen, with magic images.

I twine golden charms around your neck and a carnelian chain on your breast.

A falcon, a genet, and a *fayence* lion watch over you.

I complete your amulets with eyes and green pearls made of gemstone.

I paint an Udjat Eye on the ground so that your majesty can sleep in his interior.

I summon the gods who provide your protection so they ensure the security of your house until daybreak.

THE SELECTION OF THE HOLY ANIMAL, THE LIVING FALCON

Expert

The cult guarantees the presence of the god and the renewal of his power to work and weave. This occurs in accordance with a strict rite following the rhythm of day and night but also the annual cycle within the framework of religious celebrations.

The Egyptians believe that the gods are immediately present in their cult images but that they can also appear in the shape of a living animal sacred to them. For Horus, the sacred animal is the falcon.

Once a year, priests carry the god Horus, as represented by one of his statues, on the procession pathway out to the place in front of the pylon. There, living falcons are exhibited to him one at a time . . .

Finally, the statue of Horus inclines towards the falcon, who shall henceforth be the god's incarnation.

The decision has been made and the selected falcon is presented to the believers high on the bridge between the two towers of the pylon in the Window of Appearance.

Popular Rituals and Festivals
THE SMITING OF THE ENEMIES

Hathor

I give you, oh king, that all countries are under your control through the devotion felt by the hearts of their inhabitants. I give you that the rebels fall beneath the soles of your feet and insurgents are slashed by your knife!

Horus

I give you that your club comes crashing down on the heads of the nine-bow people.

I give you the power to kill your enemies and I make your arm strong against your adversaries.

I give you that South and North hail you, West and East bow down before you.

King

The foreigners have been cut down, the Irtiu intimidated, and the Libyans driven away from your chamber.

The Bedouins, Menetjiu, and Schatiu will be butchered once they have been seized by their shocks of hair.

King

Rejoice, Horus of the Horus gods on the Throne of Edfu! Your adversaries were felled by your knife, oh kingly Lord of Might!

THE BATTLE BETWEEN HORUS AND SETH/THE HARPOONING OF THE HIPPOPOTAMUS

Isis

Fortify your heart, Horus my son!

Pierce thou the Hippopotamus, thy father's foe!

Languish not, Horus!

Your hand is one with the harpoon!

Your ore has seized his bones!

I have seen your lance in his body.

Your horn has done solid work on his bones!
Eat the meat of his neck!

THE MYTH OF HORUS AND SETH, OSIRIS AND ISIS
Commentator A
Why this butchery?

Commentator B
Yes, a gruesome family history.

Commentator A
And that among gods?

Commentator B
Why should things be different among gods?
Like in many dynasties, no less was at stake than the family inheritance.

Of course, attempts at conciliation were made, and judgments of the court were even made before Re, the ruler of the universe. But sometimes the privilege and the power were awarded to the one, then to the other. Things endlessly went back and forth.

Commentator A
But how did it all start?

Commentator B
Seth slayed his brother Osiris and seized his royal office. Isis, sister and consort of Osiris, dreaded Seth and thus gave birth to her son Horus in a safe hiding place in the delta swamps, raising him there.

When Horus found out that Seth had killed his father Osiris and appropriated his inheritance, he swore revenge.

Commentator A

Thus the hippopotamus is Seth?

Commentator B

Yes—and every year the battle between Horus and Seth is staged in front of the temple in Edfu as a ritual performance.

Commentator A

The battle between Good and Evil!

Commentator B

Well, Good and Evil, Order and Chaos, Fear and Safety . . .

Commentator A

Fair enough, but here in Edfu the triumph of Horus is celebrated, isn't it?

Commentator B

That's right. And through this very performance the ruling king—in the form of Horus—was exalted as the powerful and able-bodied ruler of Egypt for all the world to see.

Commentator A

And the enemy was eaten with relish as a hippopotamus cake.

Commentator B

Religious festivals were celebrated in numbers. One of the largest and most splendid ones was the 'Lovely Festival of Behdet,' which took place when Hathor of Dendera, the god's and king's mother, who nourishes the inhabitants of the Underworld, the goddess of women, music and joy, visited him, Horus, her consort in Edfu.

THE LOVELY FESTIVAL OF BEHDET
Narrator C

A large festival of drunkenness . . .

Narrator A

Very early in the morning Edfu is inundated with all good things, with millions and millions of marvelous things.

Bread and beer abound in unlimited quantities, there are countless bulls and fowl which make the altars festive, fattened-up geese as burnt offerings, myrrh, incense. and chrism on the embers, which makes it impossible to see the sky above Edfu.

The ground is saturated with the green Eye of Horus, with the wine from Schefit und Imet.

Narrator C

The inhabitants of Dendera join those of Edfu, drunken from the wine, anointed with tishepes oil, and decorated with garlands around their necks.

INSERTION: WHISPERS OF LOVE
Horus

You alone, beloved, are unparalleled, more beautiful than any other woman. You are as brilliant as the rising star which announces the new year.

You splendidly virtuous, Shiny-Skinned One whose eyes are clear, whose lips speak sweetly, ushering not a word too many.

With tall stature and shimmering breast your hair is of real lapis lazuli, your arms surpass gold, your fingers are like lotus goblets.

Hathor

My beloved, my lotus flower, I come to you; it is delightful to go to the river. My wish is to go into the water and bathe in front of you.

I will let you see my beauty in a shirt of finest linen, imbued with balsam oil and my hair woven into braids.

Beloved, behold me!

Narrator A

The king's priest and the Semer priests have arrived in their festive garments.

Horus and Hathor present themselves in their procession barks, for they are departing on a journey together.

Expert

At the harbor the priests and honoraries board the ships and the crews stand ready at the oars, hoist the sails.

The journey up the Nile begins.

Narrator/expert

The ship's procession is approaching its destination: Behdet, the Godly Site of the Nome of Edfu over there on the edge of the desert, the holy place where the godly ancestors of the temple are entombed: Osiris, the Ennead, the deceased children of Re.

Hathor

Perform the ritual: tread on fish!

Let the gray geese take flight—to the south, the north, the west, the east!

Horus

Drive the calves onto the threshing floor!

Tread on the grave of my father Osiris!

Father, First of the West, Lord of the Dead!

This is the chamber of Isis, my mother, who takes you into her arms, who embraces you and joins your head, who joins together your limbs in bands, for your body was fragmented and scattered in all countries.

Hathor

I make my offering on your grave underneath the holy tree and bring wine to your Ka.

Priest

The god of the primeval ocean has stopped raging, the Nile rejoices and smoothens out its waves, the animals of the water and the crocodiles are quiet and peaceful.

Priest

The temple of Edfu, site of pleasant life, stretches out its arms to receive you again, Horus, and your face is cheerful at the sight of it!

HYMN TO HORUS
Alternating voices

Have awe of Horus-Behdety, the Great God and Lord of the Horizon.

Have awe of Horus, you gods in heaven, for he is the Perfect Sun Disc.

Have awe of Horus, you gods on earth, for he is your king.

Have awe of Horus, you gods in the underworld, for he is your sovereign.

Have awe of Horus, you men and women, for he takes care of you.

Have awe of Horus, you foreigners in general, for he is the one who wards off the enemy.

Have awe of Horus, livestock small and large, for he is the Radiant One, the sight of whose rays one lives on.

Have awe of Horus, you birds and fish, for he is the one who floods the river bank, who gives the air of life to all the living.

Have awe of Horus, you plants in the field, for he is the flood of the Nile in the form of the Thrustful Bull.

Have awe of Horus, all of you!

For he is the Primeval Father who spat out, thus bringing you to life.

Suggestions for Further Reading

The British Museum Book of Ancient Egypt, edited by A. J. Spencer. British Museum Press, The American University in Cairo Press, 2007.

The Complete Gods and Goddesses of Ancient Egypt, Richard H. Wilkinson. Thames & Hudson, The American University in Cairo Press, 2007.

The Complete Pharaohs: The Reign–by–Reign Record of the Rulers and Dynasties of Ancient Egypt, Peter A. Clayton. The American University in Cairo Press, 2006.

The Complete Temples of Ancient Egypt, Richard H. Wilkinson. The American University in Cairo Press, 2005.

A History of Egypt: From the Earliest Times to the Present, Jason Thompson. The American University in Cairo Press, 2006.

Pharaonic Civilization: History and Treasures of Ancient Egypt, Giorgio Ferrero. The American University in Cairo Press, 2008.

The Temple of Edfu: A Guide by an Ancient Egyptian Priest, Dieter Kurth. The American University in Cairo Press, 2004.

Temples of Ancient Egypt, edited by Byron E. Shafer. The American University in Cairo Press, 2005.